What are they Playing?

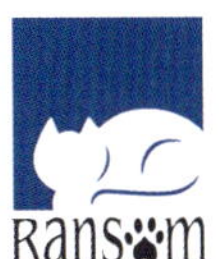

Written by
Stephen Rickard

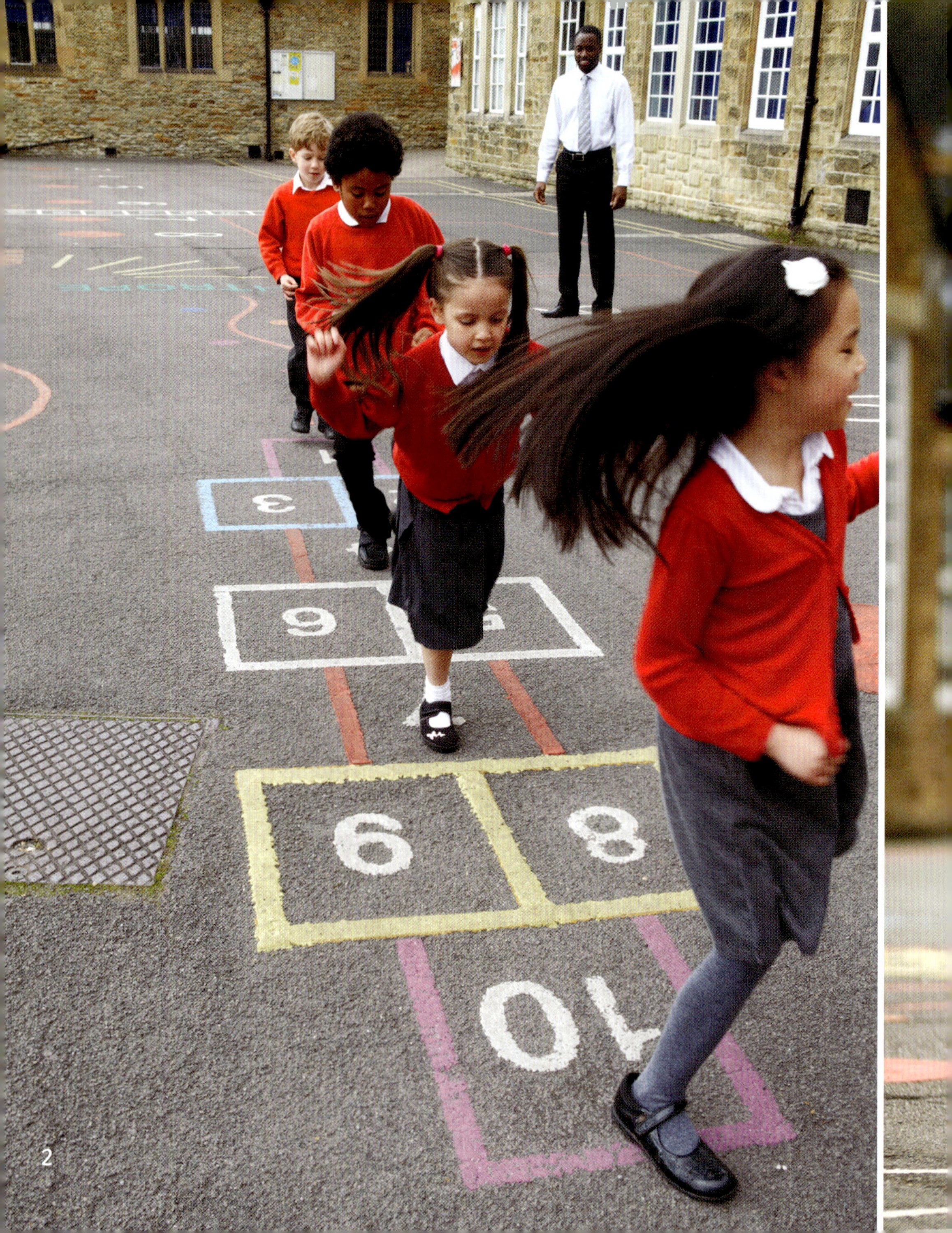

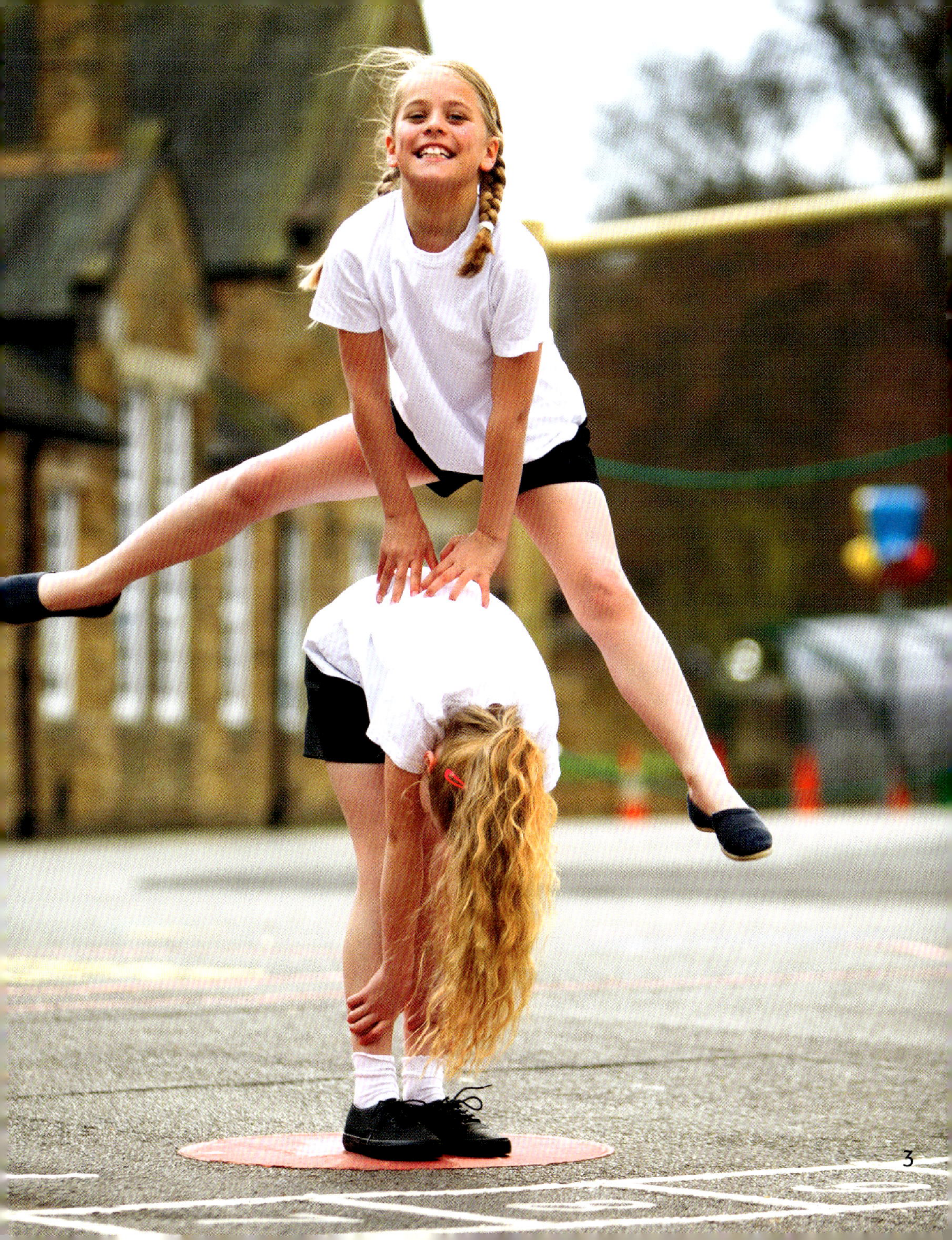

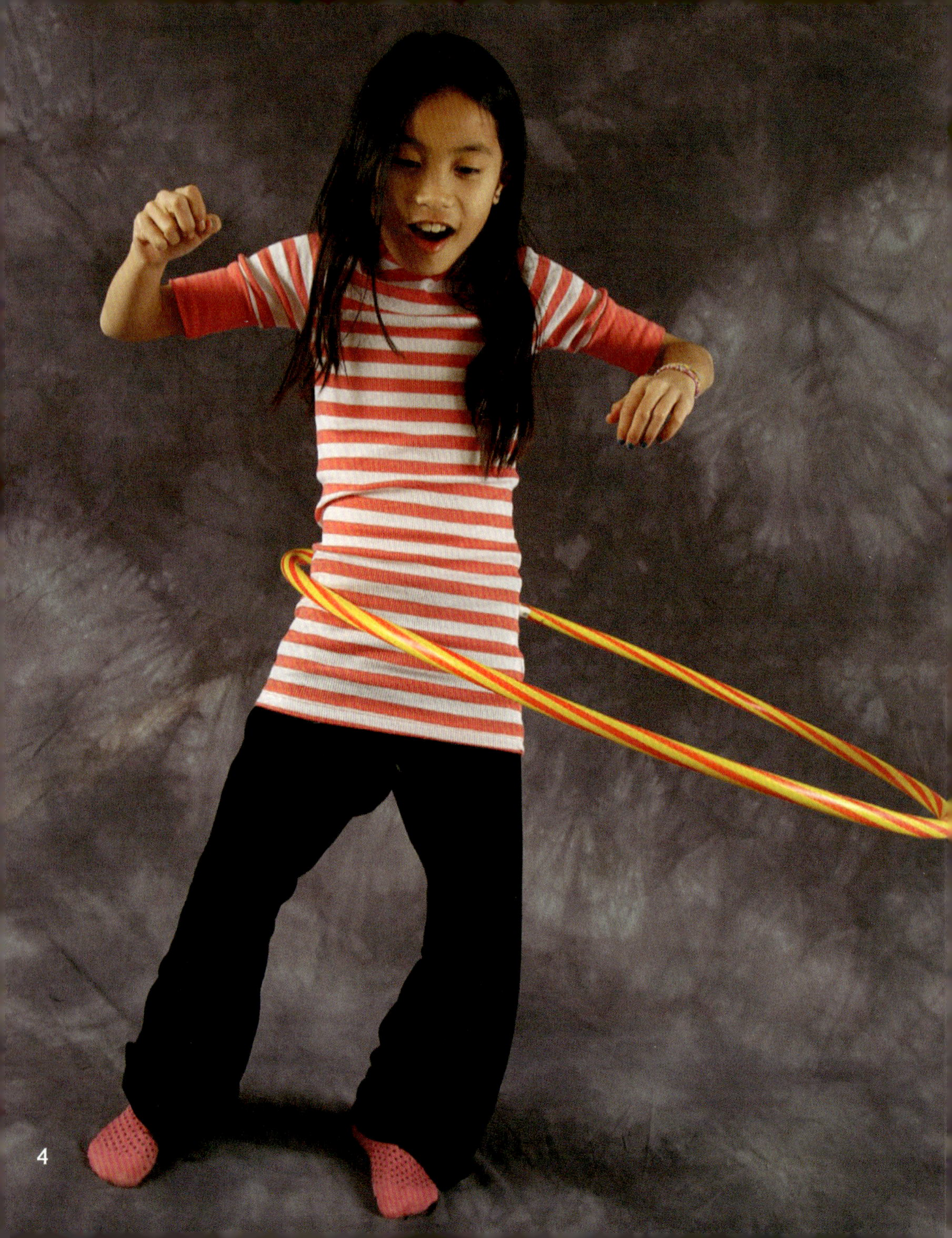

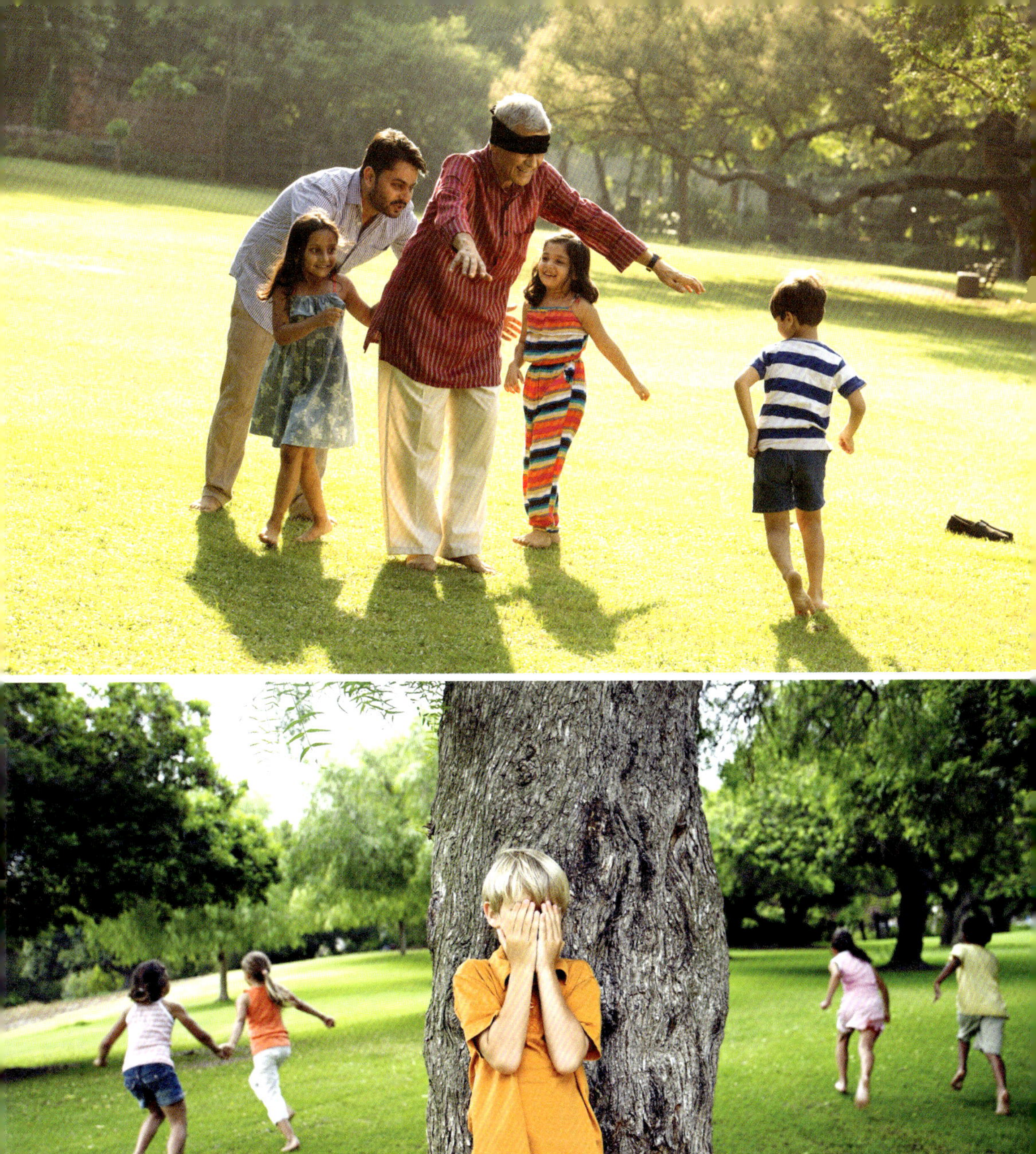

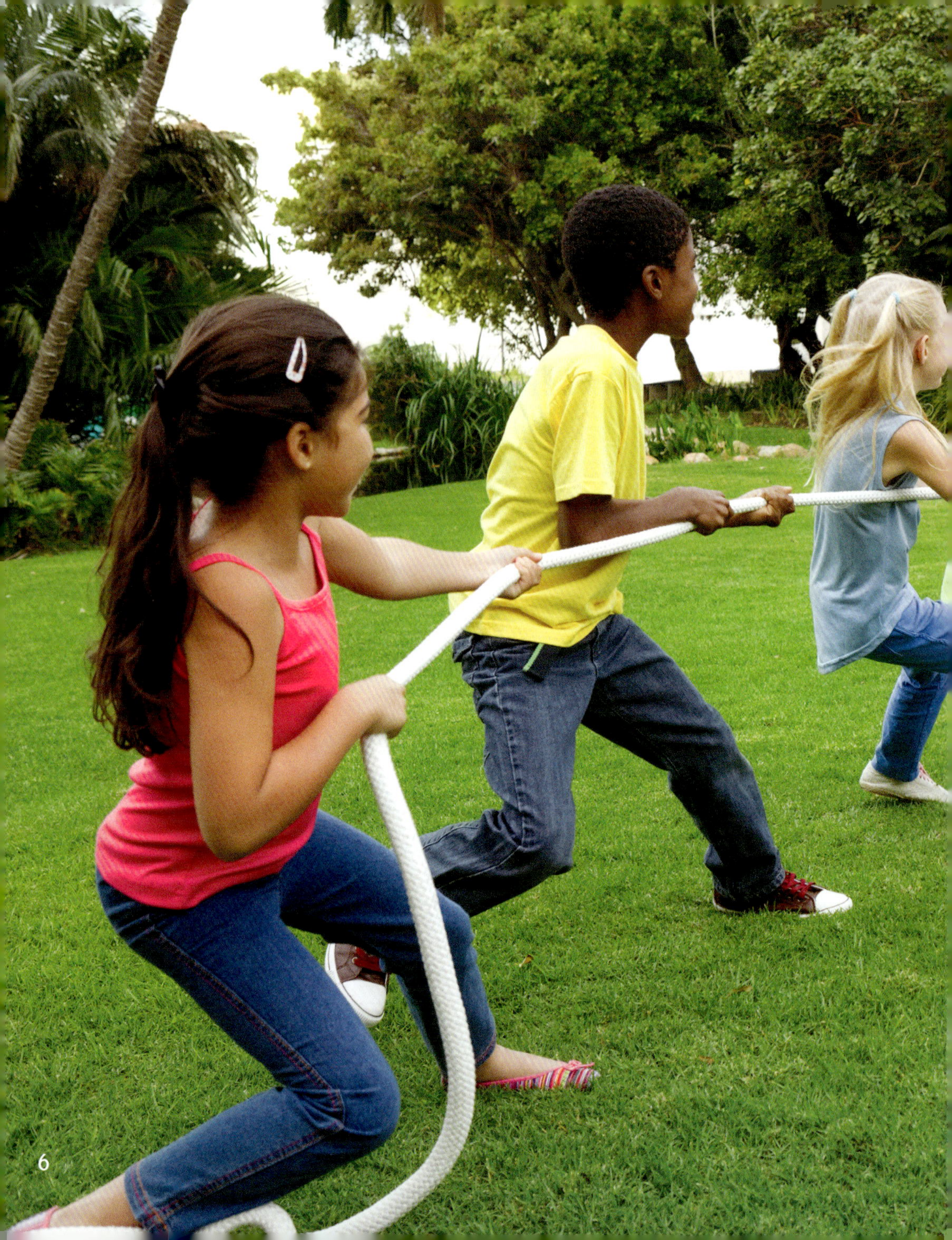

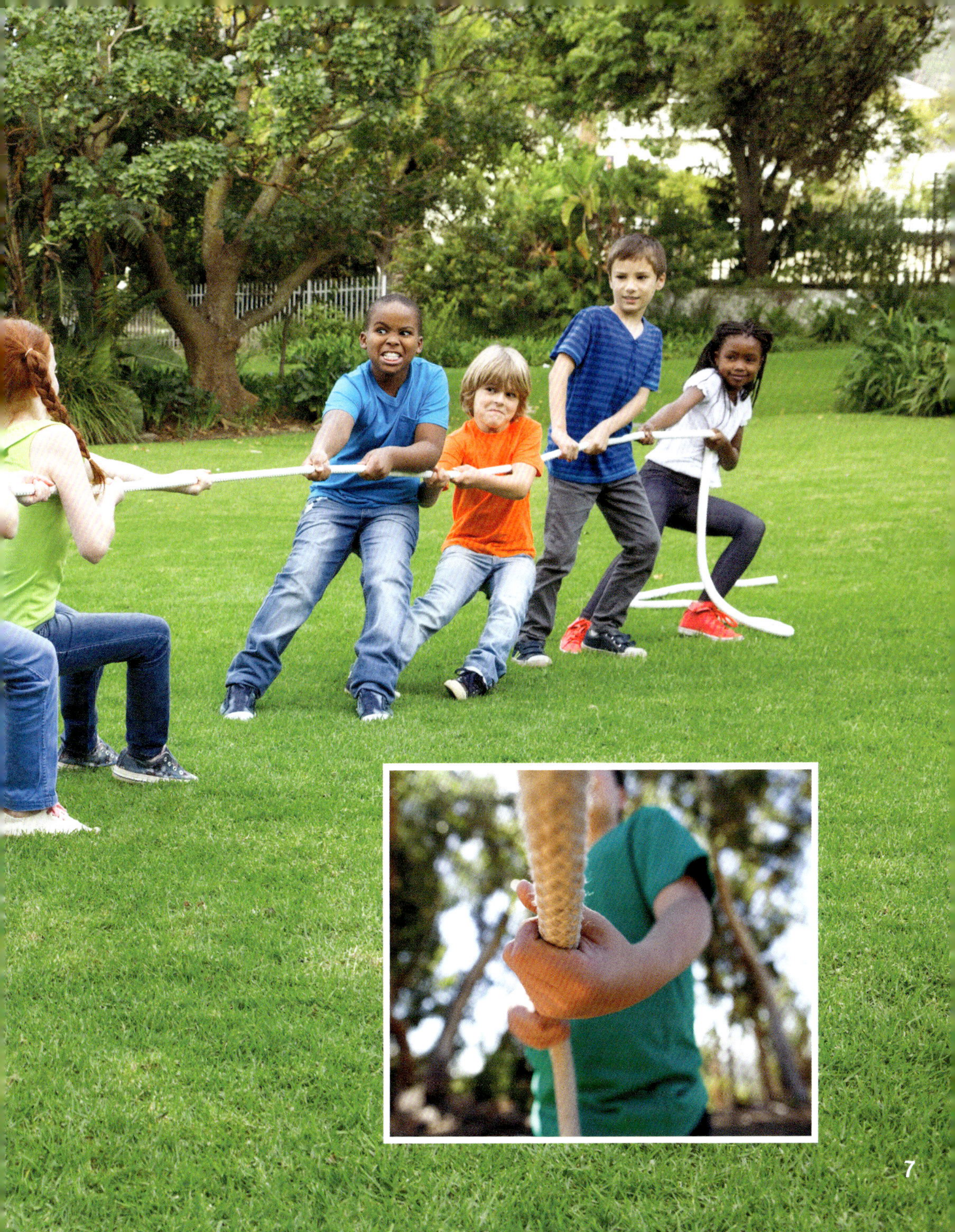

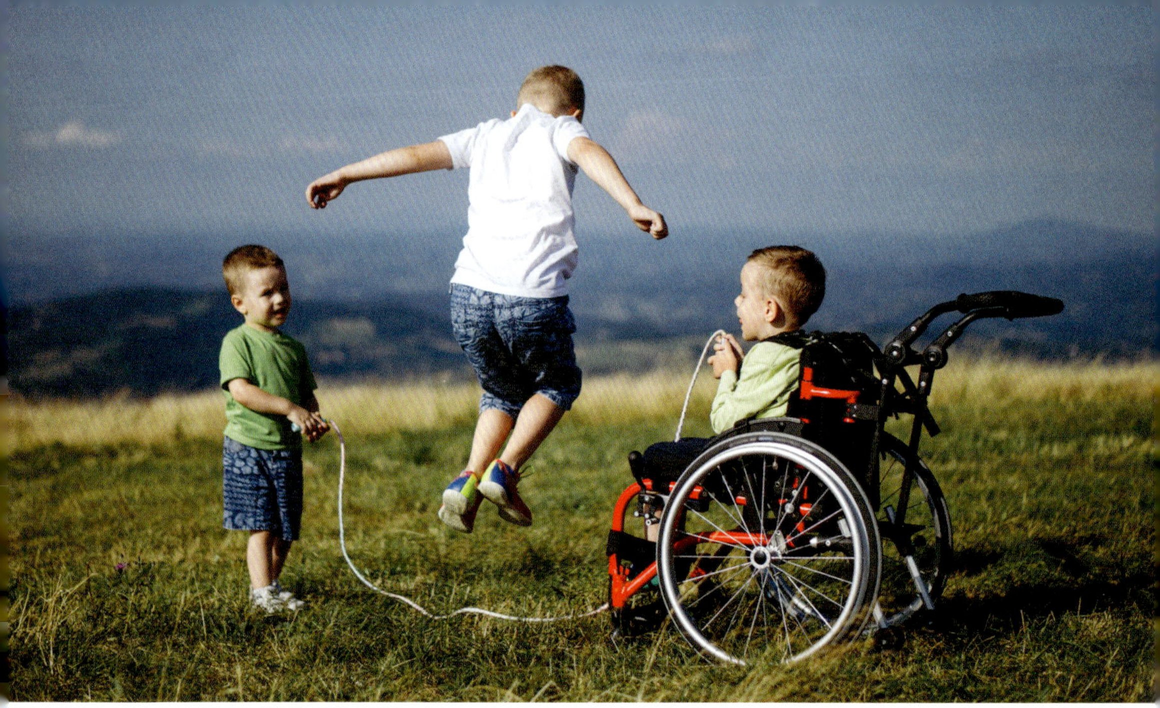

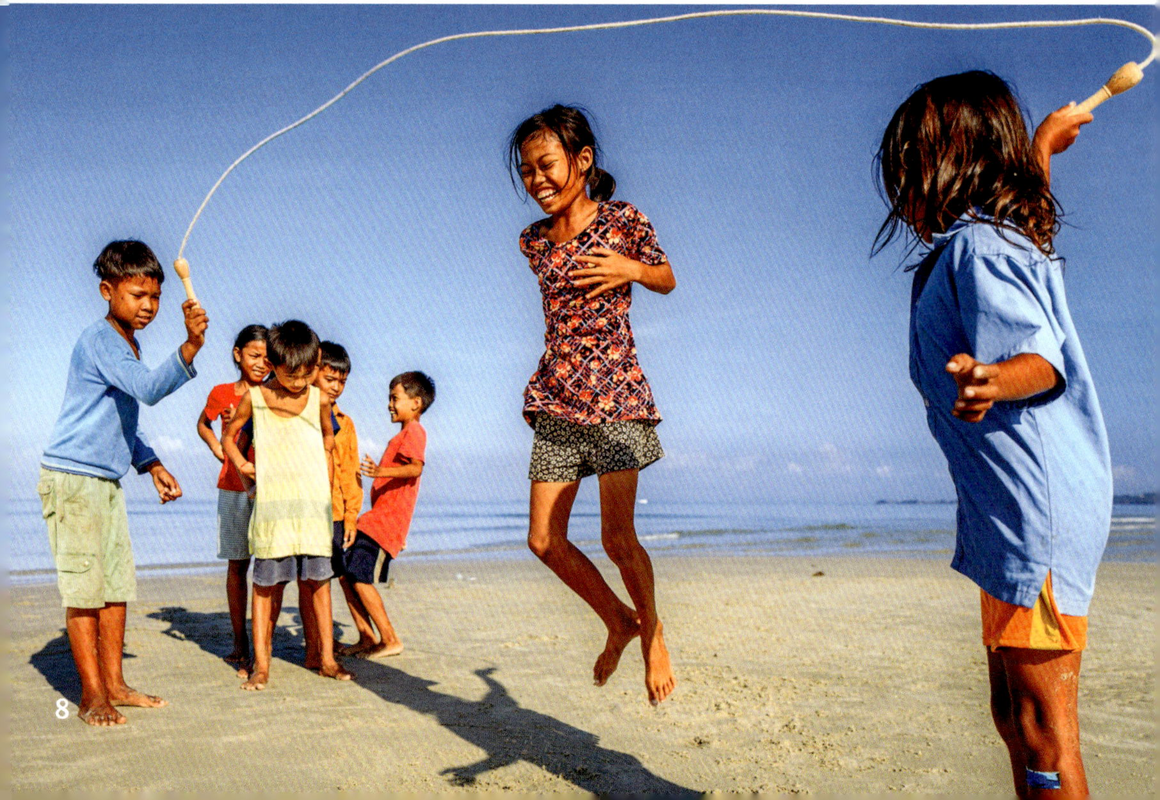